ARBORS AND TRELLISES

ARBORS AND TRELLISES

WARREN SCHULTZ

BARNES
&NOBLE
BOOKS
NEW YORK

A BARNES & NOBLE BOOK

Barnes & Noble Edition 2002

©1999 Michael Friedman Publishing Group, Inc.

Library of Congress Cataloging-in-Publication Data available upon request.

ISBN 0-7607-4120-4

Editor: Kelly Matthews
Art Directors: Jeff Batzli and Lynne Yeamans
Layout: Philip Travisano
Photography Editor: Susan Mettler
Production Manager: Camille Lee

Color separations by Fine Arts Repro House Co., Ltd.
Printed in China by C.S. Graphics Shanghai Co., Ltd.

1 3 5 7 9 10 8 6 4 2

Table of Contents

INTRODUCTION

*T*here is a basic rule of gardening, an irrefutable law of the landscape that can be called the principle of verticality. Simply put, gardens are visually improved by the addition of vertical elements. And it follows that arbors and trellises are ideal considerations for adding vertical interest, particularly since they lend attractive support to all types of clinging, hanging, and dangling plants.

Arbors and trellises can influence a garden in many ways. They can add a touch of elegance. Sometimes, they create a spot to sit and stretch out with a good book, or they might just offer a good garden vantage spot, out of the glaring sun. They can also provide privacy by screening certain areas from view or by offering a secret place for a rendezvous or just a place to escape.

In addition to creating a mood, arbors and trellises offer a very concrete benefit to the landscape: They increase your gardening space. You can squeeze more plants into the same place if they're growing up, and plants often fare better because they receive more sun. They also benefit from disease-discouraging breezes. Plants take on a whole new dimension when they're allowed to grow up—and the best way to encourage a plant to climb is by introducing an arbor or trellis.

Finally, these structures offer more versatility in the landscape. They can immediately transform a plain, flat lot into something special.

ABOVE: Designed to lift plants closer to the heavens, arbors add a new dimension to the landscape. The roses on this arbor have been raised to a special, lofty position and appear to be clouds floating above the green shrubbery.

OPPOSITE: Arbors can act as doorways in the landscape, marking the passage from one outdoor room to another. Sometimes, they draw you into a deep, dark, and mysterious place; at other times, they form the entranceway to a wide vista beyond the garden. Pass through this arbor and you will enter an enchanted room, where the scent of hanging bougainvillea fills the air, making it a doubly delightful spot to relax and contemplate the garden.

OPPOSITE: An arbor can serve as an attention-grabber to high-light a plant. This deep green arbor and accompanying lattice fence show off the *Clematis montana* 'Rybrum' in its best pink light. It's an inviting feature, beckoning passersby to stroll beneath it.

ABOVE: Trellises and roses go together like love and marriage, with trellises providing the stalwart background support for the ramblings that wander up and down throughout the years. Here, the bright, clean white of the trellis attracts the eye and creates a classic combination with the stunning red roses.

ABOVE: Sometimes a landscape setting calls for a delicate hand. When climbing plants are light and airy and you want to highlight their blossoms without competition, it's best to erect an arbor that is simple in design and material. Honeysuckle takes center stage here, rising above the iris on simple wire arbors. An avid climber, honeysuckle would creep along the ground if it weren't given a structure to climb, until it eventually found a tree to use as support.

OPPOSITE: Trellises don't have to impose to make a statement. Nor do they have to be flat and two-dimensional. With curves and inner space that add depth to a garden planting, this iron cylinder serves as a basket for annual sweet peas.

ABOVE: In some instances, arbors can be created without any construction at all. An intriguing feature for a naturalistic landscape, this allée of mountain laurel has no visible means of support; the plants have been trained to meet in an arch to form a natural arbor.

OPPOSITE: Trellises are essential for some plants. There are many vines that virtually cannot be grown without providing a good measure of support. However, trellises don't always have to be heavy-duty, engineered, permanent structures. These light-weight bamboo trellises are just perfect for temporary plants such as these sweet peas.

ABOVE: Trellises can be used for design as well as function. The ancient art of espalier enables a fruit-loving gardener to train this apple tree against a wall in a design reminiscent of a French *jardin potager*. In addition, espaliering fruit trees greatly increases the amount of fruit that can be harvested from a small area.

LEFT: Arbors and trellises can be relied upon to perform services above and beyond the call of duty. Although this postmodern structure lends an almost expected support for vines, it also functions to provide the landscape with a vertical interest, breaking up the sweeping wildflower meadow.

OPPOSITE: Perhaps best described as an arbor of distinction, a pergola adds an instant air of classical beauty to the landscape, as does the one pictured here festooned with ornamental grape plants. Noted for its sturdy columns and horizontal trellis work, a pergola is best reserved for a large area landscaped in a formal fashion.

ABOVE: When called upon, trellises can also be utilitarian. Here, green metal posts that have been run into the ground in front of an adobe wall disappear into the foliage of 'Blaze' roses, making it appear that the roses are clinging to the smooth wall. Climbing roses, which are actually reluctant climbers at best, will benefit from this encouragement but often need to be tied as well to stay in place.

ABOVE: Arbors often appear as sturdy pillars of strength, anchoring a landscape and making it seem more rooted and permanent. Here, rough, natural wood adds to that feeling of permanence while it also creates a rustic image that instantly ages the landscape. It's a perfect form to complement the wild and far-ranging wisteria.

OPPOSITE: Arbors can be striking even when the plants they feature are dormant. This *Laburnum* tunnel tempts the passerby to stroll through it, even without the flowers in bloom.

Chapter One

THE ARTISTRY OF ARBORS

*𝒜n arbor usually adds an old-fashioned, leisurely feel
to a landscape. It encourages strolling, tempts us to
slow down, to stop and smell the roses. Arbors can evoke many other
moods, however, and from classical pergolas to stark ultramodern
structures, a single arbor can help define the style of the garden.
Whether modern, rustic, Victorian, or formal, it's amazing how
much impact a single structure can have on a garden.*

*Arbors come in many varied shapes and designs. Some are
abbreviated, simple arches with vines growing over them. Others are
more elaborate structures, sometimes with long passageways beneath.
An arbor can also be designed to be a focal point or destination,
perhaps with a bench at the end of a garden path. In any case, all
must be designed so that the spans are sufficiently strong to bear
plants that can become quite heavy over time.*

RIGHT: Say the word *arbor* and something quite similar
to this arch of latticework lost in a cloud of fragrant rose
blossoms is very likely to spring to mind. The design
and material both carry a touch of England, making this
old-fashioned arbor just right for a cottage garden meant
to evoke landscapes of the past.

OPPOSITE: An arbor may serve as a garden divider.
Here, a delicate iron arch marks the path that separates
a kitchen garden from ornamental beds. The airy iron
work adds a sophisticated element to the food crops and
offers visual support not only for the vines growing on
it, but also for the foxgloves and aquilegias growing
beside it.

OPPOSITE: Arbors can be constructed and planted so that they are light and airy enough to allow other plants to thrive beneath them. This simple, modern timber arbor provides plenty of support for wisteria vines, and they, in turn, provide adequate sun protection for hosta and other shade-loving plants to flourish below.

ABOVE: An arbor can add order to a busy landscape. Here, a tumbled mass of flowers nearly obscures the stone path, but a simple arch draws the eye through the colorful jungle.

ABOVE: Arbors can work magic in the landscape and heighten an appreciation of plants. Greenery can be given a new dimension, making it diverse and full of character when displayed in different forms and shapes. This rustic arbor raises ivy above the ordinary and contrasts the vines with the formally clipped boxwood hedge.

OPPOSITE: A series of simple arches can create a memorable garden feature. Aligned along a path and covered with vines, these arches form a tunnel that opens to the countryside beyond. In the process, the structure conveys a sense of security.

ABOVE: Arbors are often at their best when the design is kept simple; the structure can then serve as a framework to draw attention to a garden element beyond. Here, this perfectly placed arbor takes the shape of an open doorway leading to the statue centered on the lawn in the distance.

OPPOSITE: Often, a plant determines an arbor's style. A simple, unbranched vine, such as this golden hops, calls for a simple arbor. This structure is actually a series of arches united in the landscape by the vining plants. By the end of the season, the arbor will have disappeared completely beneath the growth of the vines.

ABOVE: With its no-nonsense design and crisp lines, this sturdy, stately, and very utilitarian painted wood arbor brings a New England feeling to the garden, while it appears, at the same time, very modern with its straight lines and edges. With clematis growing up the posts and the cross beams holding baskets of bright impatiens, the arbor's plantings ensure color throughout the entire growing season.

ABOVE: It isn't only what's overhead that makes a successful arbor. Decorative posts can offer an interesting transition from the plants below to the plants above, and latticework is an attractive option. In this case, the brick walkway ties the scene together with a pattern that echoes the latticework of the matching posts and overhead trellis.

RIGHT: Nothing beats an arbor's ability to fully engulf a garden in plants. Here, roses are the *raison d'être* for this arbor, but the simple lines of this structure lend itself to the massed plantings around and over it. Stroll through this arbor, and you're surrounded by a richly layered scent of violas, delphiniums, and more.

OPPOSITE: A classical pergola may be a bit overwhelming in many landscapes, but that's where plants can step in to work their magic and soften a bold and perhaps intimidating structure. Here, *Wisteria sintensis* covers the weathered columns, making the pergola a bit less severe, and with the soft and scented blooms holding sway, the rest of the garden doesn't have to measure up to such a high level of formality.

ABOVE: Arbors may be works of art in their own right. This finely crafted arbor is meant to be enjoyed, not obscured by plants, and the wisteria, with its bright panicles exploding from sparse, twisted stems, shows the arbor off to perfection.

ABOVE: Some arbors are designed to complement their surroundings. Instead of attracting all the attention, they can provide a pleasant place to stop and take in the vista, to look beyond the garden and consider it as part of the greater surrounding landscape. This rose arbor provides a break from the hot California sun and creates an idyllic environment for a peaceful afternoon.

OPPOSITE: The unpainted timbers of this rafterlike roof evoke the feeling of a greenhouse without glass. It's clear that the clematis growing up the arch is the star here; there's no fancy woodwork to compete with it for attention.

Chapter Two

THE TRADITION
OF TRELLISES

*rellises are hardworking garden features that often pass
unnoticed when they are covered in a mass of foliage and
flowers. Look underneath, however, and you'll be amazed at the variety
and ingenuity that goes into these garden structures. You'll see plenty of
white lattice fans, of course, but you'll also discover that just about
anything that stands upright can serve as a garden trellis.*

*Trellises can be simple, slapped-together supports in the vegetable
garden, or they can be professionally constructed features in the garden
hardscape. Most often made of wood, trellises can also be found in other
materials, from iron to plastic. They can even be works of outdoor art.*

*Most importantly, however, trellises need to be sturdy. Their job is to
provide a third dimension in the garden, getting plants up off the ground.
These structures, therefore, must be well grounded and rot-resistant.
Practical considerations aside, a trellis can be the exclamation point that
ends a garden declaration.*

RIGHT: Annual flowers such as sweet peas and nasturtiums
call for support that's light, flexible, and easy to set up and
take down. Nylon or jute netting is the perfect solution, work-
ing in concert with the plants. Here, casually draped netting
suggests a swaying hammock.

OPPOSITE: Trellises often work in tandem with garden
walls. The wall provides the vertical strength; the trellis offers
a surface for the plants to cling to. Often, they work together
visually as well. This gardener has cleverly painted the trellis
and wall in colors that match the flowers in the bed in front
of them. In this way, the trellis becomes a unifying element in the garden.

OPPOSITE: Vines and brick make a good combination, but sometimes they need a little help in getting together. This clematis clings to the brick wall with the assistance of nearly invisible wires. Trellises are sometimes at their best when they're not seen at all.

ABOVE: This classical fan design made from time-honored materials is perfect for displaying plants at their best. The shape allows plants plenty of room to spread out and adds a whimsical embellishment to the garden.

LEFT: A trellis doesn't have to be constructed of expensive materials or be an elaborate, custom-made design. Here, a length of wire hardware cloth fastened to an adobe wall makes the perfect support for a *Senecio*. In time, the plant will grow to completely hide the trellis.

BELOW: Wooden lattice is an ideal material for trellises. The clingiest plants can hook right into the patterned notches, whereas others, such as this rhododendron, can grow right up through the spaces.

ABOVE: A rustic twig-and-branch trellis is perhaps the most natural-looking way to train climbing plants. Here, this intricately patterned trellis appears as though it has grown right up out of the garden. A trellis such as this can transform any piece of land into a bit of British estate property.

OPPOSITE: In addition to providing support for vines, this simple, geometrically shaped trellis adds visual interest to a walled city garden. The structure fits unobtrusively into the landscape, while its painted green finish warms up the cold brick wall. From a practical viewpoint, you can't beat wood as a trellis material; its surface is soft enough to allow plants to grab on.

ABOVE: We often think of trellises as old-fashioned, but this modern rendition proves that that's not always the case. The large circular space in the center of this structure provides a huge port-hole for viewing the scene beyond. Climbing vines help to soften some of the edges.

ABOVE: This basic trellis design consisting of sturdy posts and a few crossbars is all that's required to create a splendid espalier of apple trees. Allowing plenty of room for the trees to grow, this structure permits a maximum amount of light to reach all the branches.

LEFT: There's virtually no limit to what you can use as a trellis. Plants are willing growers, ready to take on just about any shape or size of support. Here, posts and chains of the type you might expect to find in a parking lot look right at home in the garden once vines have taken over.

OPPOSITE: What could be simpler than two posts supporting a crosspiece? But add some white paint and plant a climbing rose at the base and you have added an elegant embellishment to the garden.

Chapter Three

PLANNING FOR PLANTS

*W*hen all is said and done, an arbor or trellis must still play the supporting role; the real stars are the plants that grace them. Ultimately, the success of the structure depends on how well it showcases the plants. And because different vines and flowers call for different styles and materials, arbors and trellises should be planned to harmonize with plants.

A vining plant's ability to cling varies from plant to plant. Some are reluctant climbers and need to be fastened. Others cling by means of tendrils that sprout from stems, leaves, or flowers. Some have aerial roots or thorns that cling to supports. Still others twine completely around any available structure.

When selecting plants, remember that many vines are woodland plants that evolved to climb trees in the forest. They often like to have their heads in the light, with their feet, or roots, in the shade. Deep mulch, approximating the litter on the forest floor, is also appreciated. In addition, vines and climbers may be annuals or perennials; support for perennial plants must be sturdy, as the plants grow in size and weight year after year.

ABOVE: With clinging tendrils that make it an excellent climber, a passion flower adds an exotic element to the landscape. A tropical plant from Brazil, it blooms in warm climes with large blossoms that put on quite a show.

OPPOSITE: Plants are adept at making transitions. Here, *Clematis montana* bridges the gap between garden bed and building. It happily climbs from brick wall to wood trellis, bringing the two elements of this town house garden together in the process.

ABOVE: Most climbing roses are vigorous growers, with their foliage covering even the tallest trellis in a single season. Their shiny foliage is attractive even when not in bloom, but when their flowers do develop and open, they seem made to be presented as only an arbor or trellis can. Roses, however, are not natural climbers. They produce no tendrils or aerial roots, so they must be tied to their support.

ABOVE: Rich purple wisteria clusters complement natural wood. Here, this rustic trellis resembles the texture of a wisteria trunk itself. The wisteria plant calls to mind the outdoor living spaces of mild climates, but the plant is surprisingly hardy, surviving relatively cold winter weather.

ABOVE: A New Zealand native, red parrot beak is best grown as a tropical plant. It's a shrub that likes to climb, with crimson flowers resembling those of sweet peas.

ABOVE LEFT: Like all clematis, the stalks of the anemone clematis' leaves act as tendrils to wrap around a support and hold the plant up. Pictured here sporting creamy white flowers, it's also available with pink or rosy red blooms.

ABOVE: With the help of a supporting trellis, the bright purple blossoms of this *Clematis* × *Jackmanii* bring color and softness to what would otherwise be a stark garden wall. Strong climbers, members of the Jackmanii Group can grow to great heights.

ABOVE: When grown as a bush or ground cover, honeysuckle loses its full appeal. Only when it's allowed to climb on a trellis or arbor does the beautiful sweet fragrance gain full exposure to the breeze. Honeysuckle arbors are ideal when placed near outdoor living areas where their scent can be fully appreciated.

ABOVE: A shrubby vine that grows virtually anywhere, honeysuckle is such a hearty plant that it's actually been classified as a weed in some parts of the southern United States. The narrow, bell-shaped flowers may be white, red, pink, or orange, and the vines climb by twining around their support. The plants grow well in full sun but actually seem to prefer a bit of afternoon shade.

OPPOSITE: A climbing rose, such as this 'Adelaide d'Orléans', doesn't have to completely cover an arbor to make a statement. Set against this deep green landscape, the fluffy white blossoms stand out as they climb up this otherwise unadorned arbor.

ABOVE: Morning glories may be the fastest growing and blooming of all vines. The broad, papery thin blossoms come in pure white, red, pink, or blue. The vines will grow in nearly any soil and will eagerly clamber over any support, even a garden sculpture.

OPPOSITE: Roses must be carefully trained and tied to supports as they climb along the side of an arbor, seeking to reach the top. Here, the soft pink 'America' roses bring brightness and cheer to this garden walkway, enticing the visitor to continue along the path and pass beneath the light and airy arbor.

ABOVE: Jasmine is an evocative vine. While in blossom, it brings to mind warm, romantic nights on the veranda. With many admirers, its fragrance is considered one of the most beautiful of all flowers. A tender plant covered with bright waxy foliage, jasmine is an eager climber, readily rooting wherever it finds a hint of soil.

ABOVE: The twining vines of wisteria will gladly take the opportunity to grow upward. They are such natural climbers that in the southern United States they are often allowed to grow into trees. With spectacular blooms in purple, pink, or white, it's not difficult to imagine what they can do when provided with an arbor they can call their own.

OPPOSITE: Nothing beats a climbing rose for pumping out masses of blooms, and nothing is better at showing them off than an arbor. With blooms visible above, below, and through the white slats, walking through this arbor feels like being inside a rosebush.

Chapter Four

HARDWORKING ARBORS AND TRELLISES

*F*reshly painted, beautifully sited, and covered with blooming flora, arbors and trellises may seem like garden sculpture when actually they are, by their very nature, quite utilitarian. They perform specific functions in the garden, providing a surface for plants to cling to or highlighting plants and allowing them to look their best.

Some structures, however, provide even more specialized services. They can allow for an increased harvest and easier picking of fruit or make for healthier vegetable plants by providing more light and air, which discourages diseases. Arbors and trellises may also be erected with people in mind. They can bring needed shade to a hot, dry landscape, provide a lovely spot to sit and enjoy the surroundings, or create some much-needed privacy in a small yard.

OPPOSITE: There's nothing like an alfresco lunch under an arbor to fully appreciate the outdoors. In the landscape, erecting an arbor for fast-growing vines is often the quickest and easiest way to provide a shady respite from the noonday sun.

ABOVE: Where better to perform a June wedding than under a rose-covered arbor? Some, such as this structure with built-in benches, lend themselves naturally to gatherings and ceremonies, providing the feeling of being outdoors while still enclosing the party for a sense of intimacy.

ABOVE: You could set up housekeeping under this arbor. All the necessary elements for enjoying the outdoors are at hand, including a delightful swing. The table and chairs have surely seen many cozy meals by the fire; they could also be moved out into a sunnier section of the garden depending upon the season.

OPPOSITE: An arbor at the end of a boardwalk provides a perfect place for conversation. This one conveys a tropical and rustic feeling, bringing to mind island castaways. It would be hard to resist stopping here under the shady vines.

OPPOSITE: What was once an open corner of lawn has been transformed into an inviting bower with the installation of an arbor complete with a climbing rose. The structure creates a new dimension in the landscape, adding depth and a different perspective to the garden.

ABOVE: Arbors sometimes serve as physical demarcations, border markers, or landscape signs to facilitate the smooth transition from one part of a garden to another. Here, a rose arbor springs up at the confluence of two paths, uniting the separate quadrants in this lush garden.

ABOVE: Dwarf nectarines naturally take to a trellis. By growing the plants trellised in an informal espalier, the gardener can grow more trees in a given space and the fruit will be easier to pick. Stringing the branches against the trellis also opens up the plant to allow more light and air to penetrate to the center of the tree.

RIGHT: Tepees are ideal trellises for beans. Not only are they self-supporting, they also add an interesting accent to the vegetable garden. The twining vines will naturally climb the poles, and in a short time, these bamboo tepees will be completely covered by lush broad bean leaves.

OPPOSITE: This may be the gardener's equivalent of a reclining easy chair. Complete with an old-fashioned chamomile seat (a soothing scent is released when you sit down), this nook is backed by a trellis supporting vining plants and hanging flowering baskets.

ABOVE: There may not be a lovelier way to produce fruit than on an espaliered tree. Here, a single pear tree has been severely pruned for several years and tied to a simple trellis, forming a living fence. An espalier such as this can become a central feature in an edible landscape.

OPPOSITE: A shade house relies on the growth of several types of plants. Here, grapes grow up and over the walls and peak to provide shade for plants below while still allowing cool breezes to penetrate.

OPPOSITE: With selective pruning and the right support, an apple tree can be shaped into an espalier. With energy and light concentrated on them, these ornamental trees produce an abundance of beautiful blooms and subsequently bear a large crop of delicious fruit.

ABOVE: It doesn't take much to get a creeping vegetable up off the ground, giving it the advantages of better sunlight, less moisture that could rot the fruit, and easier picking. Here, plastic pipes covered in netting do the trick. Later in the season, plastic can be tossed over the frame to protect the plants from frost.

OPPOSITE: Grapes may be the perfect crop for the modern edible landscape. They're well behaved, and with just a little pruning, they'll cling gratefully to a trellis or arbor. There's also something luxurious—and perhaps a little decadent—about picking fat clusters of fruit from overhead as you stroll under an arbor.

ABOVE: The best place to find a hardworking utilitarian trellis is in the vegetable garden, and often the first crop that needs support in the spring is peas. In fact, you can't grow many varieties without some sort of supportive device. Netting strung between poles is often the easiest way.

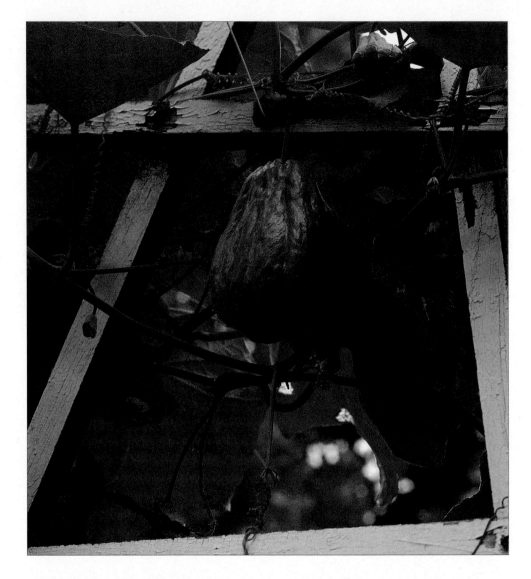

ABOVE: Vegetable garden structures are often simple and ingenious, made on the spot to suit a particular need. Although they may be light and temporary, they must also be strong enough to hold fast-growing vines, such as this chayote, a tropical vegetable that is also known as mirliton.

OPPOSITE: A favorite vegetable crop, tomatoes reap the benefits of trellis life. More plants can be cultivated in less space with fewer diseases and easier harvesting. Tomato plants can certainly be left to sprawl, but growing them vertically may be a gardener's favorite way.

PHOTO CREDITS